D1522507

THE
COURAGE
TO
LEAVE

AN AFRICAN WOMAN FENDS FOR HERSELF IN AMERICA

ADIE ALPHONTINE

CONTENTS

PROLOGUE

Leaving my native country of Gabon in Central Africa and coming to a foreign country such as the United States of America is usually perceived as a sign of achievement and as being well-off financially.

The latter, on the one hand, is true particularly if one comes from people and family who have wealth. However, what allowed me to first come to the United States of America was a wealthy lover's guilt about his infidelities towards me.

On the other hand, there is a myth that makes people back home believe that life might be without problems when one's lives in the United States of America or in any developed country. In fact, many people living in the African continent and some other countries around the world do not realize that moving to and living in a foreign country comes with its shares of difficulties and heartaches as it entails so many changes in all one's ways of life. Up until I came to the United States, I also did not fully understand the hitches that emanate from being a foreigner. After many years of living in the United States, I now, to some extent, understand this reality.

As an immigrant with no family in this country, I deal with everyday problems as well as a range of other issues on my own, which makes me feel alone at times. As a matter of fact, the feeling of "loneliness" was piercing when I was heartbroken over the loss of my oldest and youngest beloved sisters, who both died in Gabon. I am still aching and crying at times over my sisters' death, and I will continue to feel the pain for the rest of my life.

In spite of that, I have been blessed with long-term relationships with some people I have met in this country, and I consider those people "family" to me. In addition, a few of those friends have played tremendous roles in my life in helping me to be the person I have become.

Considering the ups-and-downs I have gone through in life overall and on my own since I have been living in the United States, these trials and tribulations have allowed me to be resilient and a good advocate for myself; I also have a better understanding of who I am as a human being, what things are most important to me, and a deeper grasp of the power that men still hold over women around the world.

My life experience has also helped me, to influence and empower other people in their decision making, especially when they are going through challenging moments in their lives.

In the midst of all it, my strong Christian faith has continually helped me to stay grounded, emotionally stable, and optimistic about life.

CHAPTER 1

MY TICKET TO AMERICA

At the young age of 22, I became involved in a relationship with a man from France named Alain, who owned a telecommunications company. He was twenty years older than I. At that time, in the early 1990s, I was working as a secretary for a small boating & marine GPS tracking company, also owned by a French businessman. Thus, my employer was doing business with Alain's company. One sunny workday, an hour or so before lunch break, at the request of both my boss and Alain, I went to drop off some paperwork and parts to Alain's business. At first, I thought that appointment was too close to lunch time and that I would need to take public transportation as Alain's office was some distance away from my job's location. At the same time, I did not have a choice as I had to fulfill my boss's demands and do my job. I also suspected that the appointment may have been planned that way so that Alain would have the opportunity to give me a ride after our appointment was over although, at that time, I was not fully aware of his interest in me. Indeed, all of my suspicions proved true as Alain did offer me a ride. Later, Alain stated that he had wanted this appointment at those exact hours.

All through the appointment, as Alain and I were sitting and conversing in his organized but chilly office, his eyes were staring in awe at me with a bit of spark. As I was watching him, I could form an image in my head that he was fond of me, but he did not state his interest that day.

On another day soon after, I was leaving work for lunch when I saw Alain's pickup truck parked at my workplace. He drove towards me; then, he slowed down, rolled down the window, and offered to drive me to my lunch location, which I accepted.

Since I had a girlfriend who lived about fifteen minutes away from my place of work, I always would go to her apartment during my lunch break. My grandparents' home, where I resided, was on the other side of my workplace and about forty-five minutes by car—it was way too far to go home for lunch. At the time, I was not driving and did not own a car. In those days, owning a car was still not financially accessible to many families, including mine. In fact, my grandparents never owned a car; instead, my grandfather owned and rode a "moped" during his entire adult life. In the family, we all used taxis when it was necessary to move around in the city. Moreover, the Gabonese Department of Labor had laws in place that required employees to have a break lunch from 12pm to 3pm, and the employers needed to enforce those laws. On top of that, the office where I worked would close during the lunch break. Nowadays, the workplace laws about lunch break have changed and are more like the working hours we have here in the United States.

Since there was an established professional relationship between me and Alain, it did not feel unsafe to ride with him in his car. When I was growing up, back in those days, it was unheard of for a well-known and professionally established man such as Alain to physically harm a woman that he was interested in being with and was developing romantic feelings for. During the ride, he stated that he had been looking for ways to see me and have a conversation with me. Afterward, he asked me to go out on a date on Friday of that week after work, and I said "yes." Since I was still living at my grandparent's home, I told my family that I was going to spend the weekend at my girlfriend's home, but that was not accurate. On Friday evening, Alain and I went to eat in a French fancy restaurant.

Later that night, we ended up at a night club to listen to music and dance until the early hours of Saturday. Following our night out, we spent the succeeding four days together at his home as he expressed the desire to spend more time with me. During that time, he asked me to move in with him. I said that I needed some time to think about his "offer" as I thought it was too soon and we barely knew each other in an intimate and romantic way. I felt pressured to move in with him because he only gave me a few days to think about the whole situation: he stated he didn't have the time to commute between his home and my family's home where I was residing. To further persuade me, he said "nothing ventured, "nothing gained." Last, he added, "in life we have to take risks."

When I returned home after having spent a few days with Alain, I talked to one member of my family who was my trusted confidante, my mother's cousin, about Alain's interest in me. During the conversation, she also encouraged me to move in with Alain and take a leap of faith for that relationship. So that's how it came about that I went to live with Alain although I was still hesitant to move in with him because I did not really know him. It was my first experience living with a man.

When we met, Alain was a successful businessman with charming blue eyes who was highly educated, came from a wealthy French family, had once been married, and was a father of two children ages eight and eleven. Furthermore, Alain had already accumulated a great deal of life experience; when he wanted something, he would do anything to get it.

During the first three years of our relationship, everything went well, and we both were content to be with each other. I am not certain if my feelings for him could be called "unconditional love," but I enjoyed being with him and appreciated the type of lifestyle he provided me. At such a young age, I wonder if one knows what "unconditional love" is. Even now, at this stage of my life, with more experience, I have never known unconditional love with the men I have had romantic relationships with; nor have I seen it often in the lives of people in my *entourage*. I am not certain if that kind of selfless love is ubiquitous although there are probably some people who have experienced it. Nevertheless, throughout my relationship with Alain he was attentive to my financial needs. I was well taken care of and lived a very comfortable life. Although I had everything I wished for financially, Alain was not entirely emotionally or physically present in our relationship because he travelled a lot for work and was continuously worried about his company. Consequently, we were spending a lot of our time without each other. During the years I lived with Alain, I also had the routine of traveling alone to France and Spain in the summertime to visit my friends and family who are French citizens.

Whenever it was possible, I travelled with Alain so that I would not be alone, which allowed us to spend intimate time together. Travel was fun and gratifying. Of all the European and African countries as well as Gabon provinces I had the opportunity to visit with Alain for business, I would say that our adventurous trip to Kenya where we saw wildlife was the most mesmerizing and memorable place I have ever been. Since Alain needed to attend a work conference in Kenya, he also made it possible for us to have fairy-tale moments while we were there. We stayed in a magnificent wooden lodge that was encircled by beautiful green flora. Inside the resort, there were multiple restaurants that provided tourists with different kinds of cuisine from all over the world. In addition, the resort had many souvenir shops and indoor swimming pools of various sizes for adults and children. During our two-week sojourn there, at dinner time each evening, we always ate at a different restaurant as we wanted to taste all types of food that were available.

A week or so into our trip, we travelled to a spectacular camp located in the woodland. On the campsite, our bedroom was made up of a tent hut, which had two single beds placed on each side of the room, parallel to each other; each bed was partially covered with mosquito nets, and the entire place was exquisitely decorated. At night from our beds, when the lights were off and the sky lit by the moon, we could see giraffes stand in back of the wire fence designed to keep the animals away from our tent. I was in total awe of the elegance of a giraffe's sluggish walk.

During our stay in the camp, one early morning we rode in an open 4X4 pickup Land Rover with a tour guide to explore the woodland. During our adventure in the woods, we were able to see at least seventeen kinds of animals: elephants, hippopotamus, lions, zebras, leopards, gazelles, rhinoceros—it all seemed surreal and mind-blowing.

In the last day of our excursion at the camp, in the early hours, riding along with other tourists in a van, Alain and I went to Mount Kenya for sightseeing. It was a chilly morning, to which I was not accustomed, coming from tropical Gabon where the weather rarely falls below 71 degrees F.

When we arrived at the base of the mountain, I was intimidated and overwhelmed by the height of its impressive stature and its sharp top. It was foggy, peaceful, and the sky looked so dreamy from the mountain. I opted out of hiking up the mountain because I have acrophobia. For that reason, I instead walked around the site of the mountain admiring the wildlife. I still have a vivid and striking image of our stay in Kenya as one of the finest trips of my lifetime.

Throughout the time I was with Alain, he always said that I did not have to work if I did not wish to do so; but I have always enjoyed being occupied and doing something for myself. While living with Alain, I further developed my skills as a secretary through a private professional school that I attended for two years. I also owned a miniature mom-and-pop *épicerie*. I had a young lady working for me at the store. Since she did not manage the inventory successfully and was not reliable or trustworthy, I was forced to close the store a year or so after opening.

Since Alain was quite aware of his financial successes and privileges, he always exuded an attitude of superiority towards people. This sentiment was even more accentuated toward women as he proclaimed to me that he could date any woman he wanted to in Gabon.

In our fourth year of living together, our relationship deteriorated severely because Alain started having sexual encounters with multiple women, including some of my close acquaintances. It was a traumatic and challenging season for me to go through as I watched my relationship crumbling each day. In addition to that, I also was living in fear that Alain would give me a sexually transmitted disease. All of this mayhem occurred when, in Africa, one of the deadliest sexually transmitted diseases in world history, AIDS, was emerging. Although Alain and I were still physically living in the same home, in my last year of that relationship at age 27, we were living mostly like strangers; the relationship had already reached a breakdown.

Since Gabon has laws that allow men to marry multiple women, most men feel empowered and entitled to be in relationships with multiple women even when they opt not to be legally married. Inasmuch as those laws further give men most of the power in a relationship, Alain wanted me to accept his way of living: that is, his having sexual relationships with multiple women.

As Alain viewed the whole situation and the way of life in Gabon, he did not accept the idea of my refusing to be intimate with him because of his repeated infidelities. He assumed that since he was financially providing for my needs, I would accept his infidelities and would continue to be his lover. I am certain that up to today, he must still be angry that I had the courage to leave him. I still remember his saying that I would never find a man like him when I whispered my desire to leave. Then, he would add that my life would be miserable with a man whose work schedule would be 8am to 5pm and who did not have the financial resources he himself did. For some reason, I always felt that because of our age difference, he wanted to be with me mainly to show off to his social

contacts that he was with a young and physically attractive woman. I wondered if he had ever loved me with an
"unconditional love."

When I was growing up in Gabon, sexual, verbal,
and physical abuse from men towards women were
common, and they are still happening today. Although
I had not seen such abuse in my immediate family, I
had occasions to observe it in my neighborhood when
my grandparents' male friend spent the majority of his
time fighting with his four wives. In addition, the wives
spent a lot of their time quarrelling among themselves
as they competed for their husband's favor, attention,
love, and approval. At that time, I was still a teenager
between the ages of 11 to 15, and I remember how those
fights were horrifying to witness. It was hard for me to
comprehend the notion of being in a relationship with
multiple people, especially when the women were treated poorly and were powerless. I trust that being exposed
to those experiences in my teenage years helped to form
my views on relationships, including my disapproval of
those societal norms. This is one reason I have never
willingly accepted any form of abuse from a man regardless of his social status and background.

When I voiced to some of my close friends and family
my intention to leave Alain, I was immediately regarded
as nonconforming and as someone who refused to accept
the ways of life in Gabon. Feelings of betrayal, shame,
and humiliation were consuming me because of Alain's
infidelities, and, not knowing the type of life that lay
ahead of me if I stayed in Gabon, I felt compelled to

leave. I did not want once again to hear the critiques and opinions of my family or acquaintances.

Simultaneously, as I was looking for opportunities to leave that unhealthy relationship with Alain, I was developing my relationship with God by regularly attending and being fully involved in a church ministry in Gabon. In the meantime, I had expressed to Alain my desire to study English overseas, in the United Kingdom, to enhance my career as a secretary. He was utterly and unwaveringly opposed to my decision to leave. The main reason I wanted to further my English skills was that, back in those times, being a bilingual secretary was a fast way to land a lucrative employment with an oil company and/or an internationally renowned organization in Gabon. On top of it, being bilingual in French and English was highly sought after as most people in Gabon did not possess that unique skill.

After long months in which I cogitated and prayed, Alain finally agreed to financially support me. Then, one day, I was stunned when he suggested that I go to the United States to study. In my disbelief, I said to him that the English school for eight months would be more expensive in the United States than in the United Kingdom, and he said to me, "don't worry about the cost of your education." I remember how he became even more excited for me to go to the United States than I was. Afterward, he shared with me a little bit about the state of Massachusetts where my school was located and the renowned Kennedy family which I had little knowledge of. This was a testimony of God's working behind the scenes on my behalf, and this blessing was way more than I had anticipated. I also believe it was Alain's way to try to make amends for the harm he had caused to me and to our relationship.

In retrospect, I don't regret the choice I made to be with Alain in the first place even though our romantic relationship did not last longer than the few years we had spent together. My romantic relationship with Alain taught me a lot about what it was like to live with a man in the same home as well as about love and its misconceptions. I believe things happen for a reason and, regardless of its outcome, this relationship was meant to be. Throughout my relationship with Alain, I gained a great deal because he helped me to achieve some of my life's dreams and goals. Alain is the man who financially invested the most in my life. So far, no other man, including my father, had done it.

I had never dreamed of coming to America, but in September 1997, my journey to the United States of America began.

CHAPTER 2

A NEW REALITY

Since I was not familiar with America and was not able to sustain a conversation in English, Alain, who had visited the States on many occasions as a business owner and who was fluent in English, flew with me from Libreville (Gabon) to Boston (Massachusetts) where my school was scheduled to start in mid-September. After we arrived in the United States of America, we stayed at the Holiday Inn in Brooklyn for a week or so. During those first days in the country, we spent our time visiting Boston, and he got me ready for the winter by shopping for things I was going to need for my stay with the host family.

As the days were approaching for my move into my host family's home and for Alain to return to Libreville, I was melancholy at the thought that my relationship with Alain was coming to a complete end: to acknowledge that these were the last days of our times and life together. I was voluntarily leaving a situation of financial abundance, starting a new chapter of my life alone with no English language or family in a foreign country. This new reality and these sentiments were daunting and overwhelming.

Given the fact that my journey with my host family was about to start, I was enrolled as a student at the Education First Language School located in a quiet, historic neighborhood of Brighton, Massachusetts. The school placed me with a well-off Caucasian American host couple named Kaleen and Ram. My host family's "mother" was a teacher at Lesley University in Cambridge, Massachusetts, and my host family's "father" owned an accounting business. The family lived in a fine two-story home with a swimming pool nestled by trees in the safe upscale town of Waban, Massachusetts. My bedroom on the second floor was neat and modestly decorated. I was told by my hosts that I could add some of my own decorations if I wished to do so, but I decided it was not necessary since I was going to be there for only a few months. I also had a private and relatively modern full bathroom that was well maintained, with trendy fixtures and fittings; it was agreeable not to share a bathroom with anybody else. In addition, Kaleen and Ram had a regular maid who came to deep-clean the home once every two weeks.

Throughout my stay in Waban, which lasted eight months, I had to adapt to everything including differences in food, climate, environment, people, ways of doing things, interactions with others and so on. For instance, in Gabon, the food was always cooked with a lot of spices, oil, and salt. In the States, the food was cooked with sugar and tasted sweet most of the time, which was peculiar and challenging to me. These changes made me sometimes homesick for my childhood and parts of my early adulthood in Gabon.

In my family, I am the second oldest of eight children. My mother gave birth to nine children (six girls and three boys), but one of her sons died three months after birth. Moreover, my mother also reported having had a couple of miscarriages during her childbearing age. The first four born of my family were all girls (Bree, Arin, Ina, and I), and we were raised by our maternal grandparents.

When I was about five or six years old, my mother, Damaris, left me, Bree, Arin and Ina under the care of her parents while she went to pursue relationships with men. Given my age at that time and being from a culture where children are not made aware of their parents' life-decisions, my siblings and I did not know the reason our mother had left us with her parents. Children were just children, and we were not a bit emotionally affected by our biological parents' absence from our lives, mainly because my grandparents made up for that void.

Even though my mother was living her life, she would still visit us and be involved in parts of our daily lives. Most of her visits were during weekends as she was working during the weekdays. During those visits, my mother would bring us some gifts, candies and whatever she knew would make us joyful. My siblings and I always had a blast because we enjoyed our presents and were overjoyed to spend time with our mother. Whenever it was time to say "good-bye" to us, we would be sad and asked our mother when she would be visiting again. For me and my siblings, our grandparents were our mother and father because they loved and nurtured us as if we were their own biological children.

In communications I had with my mother these days, she reported that leaving us in the care of her parents was based on conversations and mutual agreements she had with her parents at that time. Apparently, it was not an unusual arrangement in families to do so as parents wanted their daughters to be in a romantic relationship or in a marriage because it was very difficult for a woman to survive financially on her own. I also believe that a woman did not want to bring her children into a new relationship when she did not yet know how the relationship would end up. In one way, she was protecting the well-being of her children. When I look back into this situation, I would say that I am glad to have been raised by my parents' mother because she instilled in me and my sisters the family's principles and life's integrities which we all possess and live by accordingly.

CHAPTER 3

MY GRANDPARENTS

After digging into my family's history and from the information I already knew, I discovered that my grandparents were from the same tribe in Gabon, spoke the same dialect which is *"Mpongwe,"* and that they had some sort of neighborhood connection as their respective families lived in the same "quartier" called *"Louis,"*

In the generation of my grandparents, it was the norm for these folks to marry a woman or man within their own tribe as they could best understand each other when communicating, and they shared the same cultural beliefs. Furthermore, marrying close to home was also believed to be a strength in marital relationships because the families could easily intervene and resolve marital problems among themselves in a friendly manner when they happened. It is still this way as police do not habitually get involved in a family's affairs unless there is a criminal act such as a "murder" or "theft" being reported.

My grandparents were born and raised in the Catholic faith and were married in that church. My grandparent's marriage lasted until they both died, but they were separated for two years at some point while they were married. When my grandparents were living separately, my grandfather fathered a daughter (about my age) with his mistress. During that time of separation, my grandmother was contemplating divorce. As she was looking for answers concerning her separation from her husband, she visited a Catholic archbishop for advice. The archbishop told her go home and stated that he "would be praying for her marital problems." After two years of their living separately, my grandfather asked my grandmother to give him another chance: to let him come back to their home. Subsequently, she reconciled with my grandfather, and they never separated again.

In that epoch, "divorce" was not typical or easily accepted by family. I am not even certain if "divorce" existed in Gabon. I believe my grandmother agreed to give her marriage a second chance because divorce was not common, and women were financially dependent on their husbands. My grandparents had strong Christian beliefs, and the archbishop's prayers must have had played a crucial role in their reconciliation.

However, they also had strong cultural and ancestral beliefs. Those beliefs were completely different from their Catholic faith; for instance, they believed that dead people were in control of their lives and destinies. They used to organize rituals to feed the ancestors once a year and were involved in other cultural rituals such as traditional dances, consulting with the occultists, to just name a few.

In the 70s when my grandfather, who we also affectionately called "Pape," worked as an accountant for the Ministry of Finance, one of his friends gifted him with a huge piece of land in the country about 45 minutes from the "Louis" quartier where they were residing. As my grandfather's age of retirement approached, he moved his wife and us into this rustic home in the country that he had built for the family. At the time we moved there, there was no development in that part of the town—it was only woodlands around us. My grandparents also owned their house in "Louis" and put it up for rent: the extra income would help the family while living in retirement. Up to today, my grandparents' house in the city is still rented, but my mother is managing the rental.

During the time we lived the country life, during the great dry season that starts in May and ends in September, which coincides with the summertime and farming season, my grandmother Aza used to plant bananas, cassava, tarot, and other healthy food on our own family's vast land to feed our household. My grandparents almost never bought vegetables and chickens as we raised our own.

I would not classify my grandparents' income and way of living into any economic or social class because they had just enough to provide for themselves, my siblings, and me. In Gabon, people of all social classes have a tendency to mingle. In many cases, most people have a loved one or a friend who works for the government or who has an affluent job.

When my sisters and I were teenagers and were on summer break, we helped our grandmother Aza plant the food. We would wake up early, around six or seven in the morning, and go to the field. We helped in cutting the weeds, cleaning the field, and planting the food. We were very happy to participate in these processes as we learned a great deal. Sometimes the planting process was long because we were in the field from the rising of the sun to the setting of the sun. My Grandmother Aza used to have a picnic basket with food and water for us to use in the field. Since it was the dry season, which had a lot of sunny days, at times we would take breaks sitting on the ground under the trees. Mostly we were covered with dust and sweat, but we were happy to help my grandmother and enjoyed the experience.

My grandmother's face often seemed tired and overwhelmed because of the hard work in the field. At the same time, I never heard or saw her complain because of the hard labor. She appeared to always be content to work and do things to help the family. I do not recall my grandfather ever helping in the field. Back in those days in Gabon, it seems that planting was mostly a wifely duty—Grandma Aza did it to supplement the family income and to have food on the table at all times. There were times my grandmother also shared some of the vegetables and food harvested with other families and neighbors.

After their brief separation, my grandparents had a solid marriage: they cared deeply for each other. During their interaction in our home, I could see that they depended on each other a lot and were always together. When I think of my grandparents, their love story was from another time— something that I don't see much of nowadays—and their relationship could really have been described as "unconditional love." After my grandmother passed, my grandfather often expressed the desire be with his wife and was inconsolable.

Subsequently, my grandparents believed in the importance of being close and maintaining family ties with one another. While very young, my siblings and I had already learned the value of family unity and how to share whatever we had with each other. I recall how my sisters and I would cut a candy into little pieces so that we all shared. My grandmother was the pillar of our family as she was the one sustaining a solid relationship with the rest of our large, extended family. I came from a family of at least one hundred members. My maternal great-grandparents had eight children. My grandfather was the second oldest and therefore the first boy of that generation. And of course, all of my maternal great-grandparents' children had children.

When my grandmother Aza was alive, she used to host family gatherings on Sundays. I still remember these times and the happy moments as we shared meals, laughed, had disagreements, and experienced discord as family matters were debated or discussed. As a family, we relied on one another in many areas of our lives.

In my town, everybody knew each other, the neighbors playing a critical role on keeping eyes on the children and on one another. We had times when a neighbor would come to my family to ask for a little bit of salt, a bar of soap, a bowl of rice, a cup of vegetable oil and so on because they did not have these items available in their own kitchen or home. As the result of this, my family would help them by giving them what they asked for; there was a lot of sharing such as this going on among the neighbors.

Although my grandparents did not have a lot of money and were struggling at times to afford certain goods as well as to abundantly provide for all of our needs, they still extended charity to others. It was a different way of living and doing things. We were like a village caring for its own. Also, there were times when my grandmother would cook and invite a neighbor to share our meals with us.

Back in those times, my grandmother enjoyed cooking in her outdoor kitchen because she could use a wood fire to prepare food. Since we did not have a gas stove, my grandmother also used a portable propane stove, particularly when we did not have wood to make the fire. The kitchen was a very traditional outdoor space made of wood siding and covered with an aluminum roof; the floor was not cement, just plain ground. The kitchen could be dusty at times because of the fumes coming from the burning wood, but the food that was cooked on the wood fire was always tasty. My grandmother was a *cordon bleu* in the kitchen as she made delightful dishes. One of the traditional popular dishes she used to make was *Poulet au Nyembe.* She would spend hours making that dish. It is made of hard palm nuts that are boiled until tender; then, the nuts are mashed in a mortar and pestle to create a paste; after that, the paste is soaked in the water to create a red liquid mixture that is filtered through a colander. The liquid is then simmered until it becomes a thicker sauce. At this stage, the sauce is mixed with hard chicken raised on our own land without anti-biotics or hormones and cooked for at least an hour or until the chicken was tender. As the same time as the food was getting prepared, we always gathered around the wood fire, looked to see whether the food was ready to be served and be eaten.

Up to today, my mother, who inherited and lives on my grandparents' land continues the legacy of her own mother to feed neighbors in need of a meal. She is known in the neighborhood for her devotion for feeding people, including the indigent.

Throughout my childhood, I grew up experiencing a mix of spiritual beliefs. However, as the years went by and we were growing up, my grandparents implanted their Catholic religious beliefs in us.

Although we were not churchgoers, my grandparents prompted us to attend church services on special occasions such as Christmas and Easter. My grandparents encouraged us to receive all the church sacraments such as baptism, first communion, and confirmation.

At the same time, they also raised us to know about their cultural and ancestral rituals.

When I look back in those times, I think my grandparents, being from another generation, still believed, honored, and held on to the traditions that had been in their families for generations and passed onto them. At the same time, they were also trying to adapt to the modern time and new ways of living by acknowledging the presence of Christianity.

I don't believe that my ancestors in Gabon were Catholics. Christianity arrived in Gabon because of the Portuguese traders in the 16th century. From there, Catholicism established itself and gained traction, becoming the leading denomination n the year 1900. At the time I was growing up, Catholicism was the primary religion in Gabon. Nowadays, non-denominational Christian churches are dominant.

When I think of my early childhood, I am proud of where I come from and of the way I was brought up.

CHAPTER 4

———⌒⌒✧⌒⌒———

TRADITIONAL MEDICINES IN GABON AND BEING HEALTHY IN AMERICA

In Gabon, Grandma Aza had extended knowledge of traditional medicines, and she used her skills to make herbal medications that were beneficial to our family's and even our neighbors' health.

For instance, if one had fever, Grandma Aza would use tart green leaves called *Noudouwelet*. Those leaves can easily be grown in a back-yard garden. Then the leaves were washed, crushed, mixed with water, filtered, and poured into a glass. This clean liquid potion was ready for drinking. This medication was meant to be taken right away: not to be stored for days. In most cases, in a matter of a day or two one would be better or completely healed.

Another medication that Grandma Aza would regularly use is called *Noudouliet* for bowel cleaning or diabetes treatment. *Noudouliet* are green leaves that also have a tart taste. The leaves can be mashed in a mortar, mixed with water, filtered, and made ready for drinking or chewed directly in one's mouth and swallowed.

When I was a teenager, I knew a little bit about the process of making a few of the traditional treatments that Grandma Aza was making such as the ones I mentioned above. As I am no longer in that kind of milieu, I have only a limited knowledge of how to make them. I wish I would have learned more as today more people are returning to nature and using more natural remedies.

My mother is still able to make some of her own natural medicines that she learned from her mother Aza to cure some of her own maladies. I also remember Grandma Aza treating me with a homemade medication to alleviate my debilitating dysmenorrhea when I was a teenager, but I could never drink the medication because the taste was so nauseous. Then, she would say to me, "you will not get healed if you are not drinking." In the end, I could not do it, and I have been living with debilitating dysmenorrhea since then. As I am maturing in age, the pain has lessened due to the anti-inflammatory diet I have adopted over the years and the natural remedies I now use.

Back at my host family's home in Massachusetts, when the frosty temperature arrived, it was tough on me because I had never lived in the cold. During those freezing days,

I sometimes developed pain in my ears and throat. At the onset of my symptoms, I did not make the connection between them and the cold weather; it was only when my symptoms persisted that I realized that they were due to the cold. Consequently, and at the suggestion of my host family, I started wearing a hat and scarf to protect my neck and ears—unexpectedly, the pain disappeared.

I still have an image of when I saw snow for the first time: it was quite an experience to see the snowflakes coming from the sky and falling to the ground. As the snow fell, I would look up at the sky and think of the creation and the wonders of God. Although I did not like the cold weather that came with the snow, at the same time I was amazed by this new experience.

Later, in my first spring here, I developed allergies because of the pollen. This was another issue I had to deal with as I was not familiar with this condition called "allergy" prior to coming to the United States. When my allergies first appeared, colder days had faded away and had been replaced by warmer ones. At the same time, the trees were blossoming and plants flowering. On one of those days, Ram rolled down the windows to freshen the air inside the home. Later that day, my nose was running like a river, and I was not feeling well. For a moment, my host family and I thought that I had caught the "flu." As I was uncomfortable and complaining, they took me to the urgent care clinic. After consultation, the doctor told me I had "allergies."

I felt ignorant while I was learning more and more things about myself and my body. When I look back at this incident, it seems to me that Kaleen and Ram also were not able to pinpoint the causes of my symptoms as they did not have information about my health history.

The urgent care clinic was not so different than the ones in Gabon as we also have private and public health care. In Gabon, people who can afford it have a tendency to go to clinics because the care is often better and quicker, but we also have a few renowned public hospitals that are very good—the only downside is that they can be crowded, resulting in longer wait times.

Since it was allergies that prompted me to go to the clinic, I believe that if I had had that condition in Gabon, my grandma would have made a home medication to ease my symptoms or cure me. I would not have gone to the doctor. When I was growing up, I barely went to the doctor unless it was something grave or something that my grandmother would not have been able to cure.

Once, my grandmother told me that I had suffered a health-threatening illness when I was an infant, and she took me to the hospital. While we were at the hospital, the doctors stated that they could not diagnose my illness. Therefore, they could not help. In her despair, my grandma took me to a family friend who used traditional medicines to cure maladies. In that case, I was cured. I have never known the details of the illness I had suffered, but my grandma always said to me that she was forever grateful for the "traditional doctor."

When I went to the doctor for my first yearly checkup in the United States, the doctor stated that I was "underweight." At that time, I did not know what it meant to be "underweight." As the doctor explained what it meant, it seemed outlandish because I had never been labelled in such terms. My father was skinny, and I thought I had inherited my body type from his genes as I was always skinny when I was growing up. People in American used to ask me if I was eating and was I a model. I have never felt that being skinny was a health hazard.

This new approach to health was another learning time of my life: so many new terms and situations were unfamiliar. This was another circumstance that reminded of the cultural variances I was undergoing as an immigrant. I certainly believe many immigrants may experience something similar depending upon of their countries of origin.

CHAPTER 5

FAMILY DYNAMICS AND CULTURE IN GABON AND USA

In Massachusetts, my host family were kind and caring and always attentive to my needs—especially the host lady Kaleen, who was great. Kaleen and Ram were parents of two grown children (a girl and boy) who were already living on their own and had left the family home to live in other states. I had the opportunity to meet and interact with them at holiday gatherings such as Christmas and Easter. In fact, as a family, we all went to Florida at Christmas time to visit with both Kaleen's and Ram's parents who lived in different cities in sunny Florida. While we were in Florida for a couple of weeks, we would spend one week with Kaleen's mother. Then, we would travel to another city to spend another week with Ram's mother. Both Kaleen's and Ram's fathers had already passed away. In Florida, we had a great vacation: my first trip outside of Massachusetts during the winter.

My interaction with my host family's children was amicable although I was not close to them and did not know them well. The fact that they were older than I and that I was not yet able to communicate fluently in English with them made our conversations very limited. I also thought that my host family's son was a quiet person in comparison to his sister, who was a little bit more engaging. Otherwise, the family's dynamic was nice; everybody was kind and helpful to me. Although I enjoyed being with my host family, at the same time, they were still people that I only had known for a short period of time, and I was still getting used to living with them. Given the way I was brought up and my culture, when I am around people who are not blood-related to me, there are boundaries I have to respect and caution to take. Coming from a large family, I was used to being in an environment that was always dealing with many issues of all sorts and was always lively. In my host family, as it was only Kaleen and Ram, the family dynamic was relatively noiseless. I left an extended family environment to immerse myself in a nuclear family. The family dynamic and atmosphere were not like any I had experienced in Gabon. Despite such a difference in ways of doing things, I still considered my host family as I did my own family, and we experienced many activities together.

During my stay with the family, we visited new places, went to concerts, spent holidays with their family and children, and they helped me with projects I had planned to accomplish. For instance, when I was looking to further my schooling after English school, Kaleen helped by providing information about the business school I was interested in attending. The fact that Kaleen was a college teacher was a blessing to me. Although the culture, food, healthcare, and environment were different from what I was used to, my host family always tried to accommodate my needs to the best of their abilities. Yet, I could not help comparing them to my own family structure and cultural background in Gabon.

Back in the days before Gabon gained its independence in 1967, it was a French Equatorial colony and, thus, the Gabonese were automatically considered French citizens. A few years after Gabon's independence, in the morning hours of a dry and cool summer, I was born at the General Hospital. It is one the oldest health-care community centers along with Albert Schweitzer's Hospital in the country. The hospital provides health care to the entire Gabonese population regardless of income and social status — its buildings are ranch-style brick houses painted in white like a military barrack scattered around a huge piece of fenced land giving it the appearance of a small village. After a laborious delivery, I am told that my mother rested in her hospital bed, dressed in a multicolored print gown. My young mother, so it goes, was overwhelmed by joy, carrying me in her arms, breastfeeding me, and caring for me. In my family's traditions, a young mother is required to rest for a few months at home after giving birth. Therefore, a family, in most cases the grandmother, will care for the infant with bathing, bottle feeding, and consoling when needed.

In Gabon, at the time I was born, women gave birth naturally with no medication to ease the labor pain. Sometimes the process of giving birth would take long hours and even days depending on the woman's readiness. From what I saw when my mother was pregnant with my younger siblings, she was given homemade remedies that were prepared by my Grandmother Aza. These homemade remedies did have the ability to ease my mother's pain before and during delivery as well as help her have living, healthy babies.

Mostly, as I've said, I was a happy child. During the summertime, my family used to go to the beach house owned by my aunt (my mother's sister) at Cape Santa Clara for a few weeks. The beach house was an hour's drive from the location of my grandparents' home, and the roads sometimes were muddy, especially after it had rained. At times, small cars got stranded on those perilous roads. While driving, we were surrounded by nature, and everything around us was quiet. I always wished for us to arrive safely at the beach house because everything around us was just forest and vegetation—it was hair-raising.

Nevertheless, I remember how we used to play on the beach and even in the forest with my friends and siblings. Since we were raised by my maternal

grandparents, we had a lot of freedom and little super-
vision. My maternal grandparents allowed us to play in
the woods and neighborhood and at our friends' houses
without fearing that something bad could happen to us.
My siblings and I grew up playing outdoors all the time.
When we were out playing, there were days when we
made small fires on our own and cooked food we took
without permission from my grandmother's pantry.
After the cooking was done, my friends and I shared
and ate the food. It was fun and creative to do so. We
sometimes just walked in the woods, exploring, and
eating different fruits we would come across without
thinking of health hazards. At that time, we were not
even aware of the danger we were exposing ourselves
to just by venturing into the woods on our own. My
friends and I were fearless because of our innocence.

A surprise occurred when I was eight: my aunt (my
mother's sister), who is now a widow and currently res-
ides outside of Gabon, took me to live with her and
her family. I believe that she took me from my mother
because she wanted to help my mother who did have
eight children to support while my aunt only had three.
In addition, my aunt and her husband were financially more secure than my mother, who was single. My
mother was not completely devoted to my and my sib-
ling's childhoods, but I believe that she did the best
she could with what she knew at that time. During
her entire career, my mother worked as a secretary for
a well-established and renowned high school, but she
never made a decent income.

I also believe that my aunt took me under her care because my Grandmother Aza asked her to help raise me as there were already Britt, Arin and Ina living with my grandparents. From what I can recall, I was told that I was going to live with my aunt because she and her husband were to provide me with better opportunities for my future. My aunt lived in a great neighborhood and lived a life that was different from the one I had when living with my grandparents. I attended one of the best primary schools in Gabon at that time and was able to travel with my aunt's family to France one summer. Although I was living in an environment where financially I was cared for, at the same time I remember that I was not happy living with my aunt and her family. I missed my siblings. My aunt did not treat me as one of her own children. I did not feel like I belonged.

After a little over one year or so of living with my aunt, she returned me to my grandparents' home because she did not want to continue raising me. Up to today, I am not sure why. I can only assume that because I was not her biological child, she did not ultimately have the desire and patience to care for me.

In the present day when I reflect upon that situation, I do not know what to think of her actions because I was only a child and in my developing stages of life. Today, I believe that if my aunt was not mentally equipped to care for me, she should have never taken me from my grandparents' home. It has also crossed my mind that she took me to show off to the family that she was rich; however, she lacked patience and a mother's unconditional love for me. As an adult myself, if I decide to care for a child who is not biologically mine, I do not believe that I will just give up on that child because he or she does not act in the way I expect: a mother who truly and unconditionally loves her child or children would not give up on them at any cost. I eventually came to realize how important it is for a child to know that she is unconditionally loved, and how painful it can be to be rejected by those whom we trust to take care of us.

There are times I think about that event and still cannot fathom the motivation behind my aunt's not wanting to keep me with her. At that time, her action created a malaise in my family: my grandmother repeatedly blamed me for not having been a good enough child while living with my aunt. Over the course of the months following this episode, my grandmother would say to me, "You have missed an opportunity to have a better future." At age eight or nine, I did not understand what she was talking about, but those damaging words have remained and sometimes keep reverberating in my mind even after all the years that have passed. As an adult, I reflect on that event in my life, and I better understand how important it is not to say harmful words to a child because we never know about the emotional damage that such words can have over the course of their life.

CHAPTER 6

HARSH AWAKENINGS

When my mother was a young woman, she was physically very attractive and always had a pool of men who were interested to date her. She is a woman who has a boldness in her character and can be unapologetic in the way she does things and conducts herself. She has shared with me that she met my father through a friend of the family who knew him and introduced him to her. She has never stated whether she was ever physically or sexually assaulted by a man. From what I observed when she was in relationships, she always was with men who appeared to be gentle and not argumentative at all. In fact, my father was a soft-spoken person. Although my mother and my father had children together, they were never married and barely lived together. Because of the type of relationship my father and my mother had, I grew up not knowing much about my father's side of the family.

When I was growing up, like my mother, I was popular in school with boys and men. Men started to be interested in my physical appearance at age thirteen because of my good looks and slender stature. Although I received a lot of attention from men, I kept myself away from these predators.

In my grandparent's home where I grew up, sex and sexual activities were not discussed. My grandparents were from a different generation and these types of topics were forbidden. The only times I had conversations or talks related to sexuality were with my girlfriends at school. I also tried to educate myself on the topic of sexuality mainly through romantic novels, watching television, and with my peers. On a side note, I was an avid reader of romantic novels, and my girlfriend and I would exchange them on a weekly basis. I also believe that reading such novels helped me to build strong French language skills.

I finally started going on dates at age 17 with a young man from my neighborhood who was 19—we both were in high school. After dating this young man for a while, I got pregnant by him. Neither of us knew anything about birth control. Since both of us were adolescents, immature, and living with our respective families, the young man decided that I should abort the pregnancy without my family's knowledge or his. Neither of us had financial or emotional support from our families—we were both on our own. I did not know what to do; I felt scared and alone. Since my boyfriend and I were at the crossroads, he and another girl with whom he soon started having another intimate relationship procured for me a medicine from a traditional doctor that allowed me to abort my pregnancy. Up to today, I don't know what that medication was made of: it looked like a small white ball, about the size of an egg or lime.

A few days after taking the homemade medication by inserting it into my vagina, I was in excruciating pain, crying in my bedroom. I was still afraid to communicate with my grandparents about my condition. However, I was feeling worse each day: I could not walk upright, and I did not smell good in my intimate parts. I started to panic about what was happening to me. The fear of dying was sinking in. I had to tell my grandmother the reason I was sick. She became very alarmed and called another family to come pick me up and take me to the hospital. It became an immense family issue because they all blamed me for what was happening. My family told me that my life was going to be hell with a baby and that I was a disappointment. I felt sad and demoralized.

Throughout the time I was at the hospital, I was told by the medical staff that my health condition was critical and that I could have died if I had not sought medical help. Therefore, I stayed in the hospital for a few weeks. During the time I was hospitalized, I never received visits from my boyfriend or his family. My boyfriend's family did not care about me; they never gave me support. He probably never even told them. In the end, all the medical expenses were paid by my family.

After my release from the hospital, I was angry with my boyfriend and his family because they did not help at all or even care. Even now, I still struggle with the pain and guilt this situation caused in my life. This experience transformed me emotionally. Afterward, I did not want to have any further intimacy with that boyfriend as he did not respect me in so many ways.

When it comes to my love life, this episode greatly shaped the way I choose a romantic partner now. In addition, it also cemented my determination not to have another relationship with a man from my own country of Gabon because I felt so abandoned and emotionally abused by that first love of my life.

At age 19, I was still living at my grandparents' home. I was soon to experience another loss. My grandmother had contracted malaria: during her entire life she had worked hard, and she was not feeling well for a few days. Soon, she went to my cousin Mousa's house in another city to be close to the family's doctor and to receive treatments. On the day that she left her home, husband, and us for my cousin Mousa's home, she said to us, "I will be back soon." Unhappily, she never came back home. A few days after her arrival at my cousin's home, she died in her sleep in the middle of the night. It was said that her cause of death was cardiac arrest due to fatigue from malaria. The night of her passing I had a dream that she had died, and I found it to be true that morning. The passing of my grandmother was deeply felt in the family and the community as she was loved and appreciated by our entire extended family. In some ways, for us, her grandchildren, we felt the loneliness of a huge void.

After my grandmother's passing at age 67, I continued living with my grandfather and took care of him until I was 22. Afterwards, I left and moved in with Alain. Then, my mother took over the care of her father. Although I had left the family home, I still continued to visit and care for my grandfather, who was always sad about his wife's passing; he had lost the desire to live. After more than fifty years of marriage to his wife and being so attached to her, my grandfather Pape was not able to sustain a long and happy life alone.

Ten years after the passing of my grandmother, my grandfather was diagnosed with late-stage lung cancer at age 77. Although Pape went through a long and painful cancer treatment to ease the pain in his body, he died when I was 27, only a few months away from my departure to the United States to study. I always felt like he did not want me to go away because he was so attached to me. In fact, I was the one who was taking him to his doctors' appointments and still caring for him even though I was living with Alain. The family who was at the hospital at the time of his passing stated that he had asked for me. At times, I have wondered whether I would have had the strength and courage to see him leave this world; perhaps it was better that I was not present.

My grandparents' passing, for me, Britt, Arin, and Ina, felt like we had lost our own parents. At that time, the grief was unbearable, but our grandparents remain present in our thoughts and memories.

During the year my grandmother died, at age 19, I was still a student, and I often went to the beach to study. I would go there because it was a quiet place where I could find inspiration; it was calming to me. In addition, my family's house was located only about 30 to 45 minutes' walking distance to the beach.

One sunny and warm weekday afternoon, the beach was peaceful as usual and there was almost nobody else there besides me. I was studying inside a bungalow when I heard voices. Suddenly, a group of three men approached me, displaying a knife and threatening to kill me. I was attacked physically and sexually assaulted. I was not able to scream or do anything about it because I was paralyzed: literally in fear of losing my life.

After the incident, I reported the crime to my family, a good friend of mine, and to the police. Nevertheless, these men could not be found. A few months later, I heard that one of the criminals had been arrested, but I did not know what really happened to him after the arrest. For the others, I don't think that they were apprehended as I was never informed about the development of the case. From what I can recall, law enforcement was not eager to spend time and resources on these types of crimes. The system, as I remember it, could be biased against women. I am not certain if there were laws that protected women against abuse and other domestic crimes. Even if the laws existed, I do not recall them being put into practice by the judicial system.

After that horrible experience, for years I lived in fear of being attacked again. A good male friend of mine, whom I considered as a big brother because we grew up together in our neighborhood, and who was a confidant as I shared my story with him during this devastating time, was very upset and wanted to take justice into his own hands. I was not certain what my friend would have done if he had known the identities of these criminals and evil human beings. I just did not like the idea of his fighting criminals on his own because I was worried about his safety. After going through such a horrible and terrifying incident, I was shattered and devastated. The fact that we did not know if justice would ever be achieved by the Gabonese authorities added to the emotional stress on me and him because he cared a lot for me. The fact that he felt that he could not help me was tortuous to him. He remains a family friend still in my life today although he is in Gabon.

Unfortunately, the abuse did not end there. Around age 21, I was friends with a girl that I knew from my school. During our friendship, I would go to visit her in her house. One day, she introduced me to her brother who was at least 15 to 20 years older than I. During the course of my visits, her brother started showing sexual interest in me although I was not interested in him. On one of my visits, the brother forced himself into me without my consent. I was once again sexually assaulted by a man, but this time it was by my girlfriend's brother. When I left that house, I had a great deal of anger and disdain for that man because he had done something horrible to me without my consent. At the same time, I felt that my girlfriend was also complicit because she knew of the sexual interest her brother had for me but did not protect me. Despite the probable disinterest of the police, I would have pressed charges against that man, but I did not do so because the incident happened in my girlfriend's house. The police would not have believed me. I am certain that it would have been their word against mine. Furthermore, I did not want to dwell on this incident as I was already in pain and feeling ashamed of what had been done to me.

Given the history of the judicial system in Gabon and the lack of interest by law enforcement and the culture in general for cases such as these, I had to deal with this situation on my own emotionally and physically. I ended my friendship with that girl because of the rancor and disdain I felt for her and her brother. On top of everything, this incident resulted in another pregnancy, which I was forced to end at a private clinic. Unlike the first time, I went through this difficult experience alone. Because I came from a culture where family dilemmas and secrets were not often openly discussed and because of the personal anxiety of going through such hurt and not wanting to hear detrimental remarks made against me, I never talked about this incident with anyone in my family or with a friend.

As I was going through this period of grief, shame, and guilt, I was at such a loss that once again I started seeking God for comfort and help. Throughout that time that I was crying out to God, I started developing a fervent relationship with Him through prayers and meditations.

This type of trauma remains in one's mind forever; sometimes one does not want to think of these experiences although life's situations can trigger those memories. It is like one wants to forget but that never happens, no matter what you do.

CHAPTER 7

FENDING FOR MYSELF

B ack in Boston, I was also not able to adequately communicate with anybody, including my new "nuclear family," but for a very different reason: my English was very limited. During dinner time, the family and I would use the English dictionary to find words to verbalize my thoughts and opinions as well as to converse with them. As Ram had studied French in high school and remembered a few words, he was always trying to find ways to help me with the translation between French and English, but it was not easy for him as his knowledge of French was also very limited. Yet he tried. In contrast, I thought of my own father in Gabon.

Growing up apart from our father, Paul, my siblings and I never developed a solid relationship with him and his side of his family. He was not involved in our upbringing and was not interested in being present in our lives. My siblings and I did not love our father as we did our mother. Back in those days, I am not sure if it was common in Gabon for a man not to take care of his biological children. I was not of an age to understand such a complex issue. I believe that if my father would have wanted to be a part of our lives and a caring father for me and my siblings, he would have done it. There was no excuse for him not to do so. Nevertheless, he chose to marry another woman and have another family of his own with his wife. My father's wife did not want him to have a relationship with me and my siblings. From what I could recall, my father also alleged that one of my sisters was not his biological child because, most likely, he did not want to pay child support and assume his obligations as a father. He worked as a police officer during his entire professional life and was financially secure because of his rank. By the time he retired, he was a colonel. On top of that, he also had invested in some real estate that provided him with a relatively decent income in comparison to my mother and my grandparents, who did not have much.

Although my father and mother kept up an amicable relationship when we were little, my mother did not talk to my father's wife because she believed her to be the one responsible for the dissolution of my father's and mother's relationship. I remember how my mother was upset about the entire situation. She always stated that my father's wife used occult power to influence my father's decisions and mind so that he could not clearly think and make rational decisions for himself. As I have said, some people continue to believe that the dead and ancestors still have influence over one's life.

At the age of 15, one day I went to visit my father who worked for the Defense Ministry. For one to get into the building and offices, it was mandatory to show an identity card to the guards at the doors. Once the guards had your information, they would let you go see the individual you wanted to see. My father was often surprised to see me because there was no way for me to inform him in advance of my visits. We did not have cellular phones and social media platforms. I normally saw him two or three times a year to ask for financial support as he was not involved in my life and not paying child support to my mother. During our conversation that day, I stated to my father that I was in need of financial assistance. He replied to me by saying, "You are a young woman now and you should be able to take care of yourself." After my visit with my father, when I went back to my grandparents' home, I was shaken and upset as well as disappointed by my father's words. I could not believe that my father was asking me to "take care of myself."

This experience stayed with me through the rest of my adolescence. Even now, I sometimes think about what he said to me that day. There are times when I still cannot believe that a parent would ask their teenage daughter to fend for herself. And yet perhaps it was good advice, for I have often had to do so.

In America, I was always fending for myself and worrying about my "better future"; it was far from easy. When I was going through all the struggles and issues of being a stranger in a new country, I always was asking myself, "why did I come to this country?" I had always thought that I was going to be here for just the duration of my English studies and then permanently leave America, but that was not to be.

While I was living with the host family and not in possession of a driver's license, I used public transportation to go to school and other places I needed to go. One fall morning, as both the temperature and leaves were falling, I rode the train on my own and went to a subway station in downtown Boston to buy a monthly pass. When I was at the subway station in front of the cashier, I was not able to communicate with her because I did not know how to say in English, "I would like to buy a monthly pass." While standing in front of the cashier, I heard her talking to me in English, but I did not understand what she was saying to me. Suddenly, I just decided to leave the station without buying the pass—I was frustrated and angry at myself.

During that period, I remember practicing my English at all times, always preparing my speech beforehand, so that when I was meeting people, I knew what to tell them. Then again, most times, I was not able to adequately express my own thoughts as I felt intimidated by the fear of being judged. The fear of expressing myself took me many years to overcome.

These frustrating experiences with people were always hard on me because I could not interact with them and could not be helped with whatever I needed. At times, I was discouraged; I felt uneducated because of my inability to communicate in English. During the time that I was going through the adjustment of being and living here, there were days when my feelings and thoughts were all over the place about my sojourn and future here—my mind was constantly at work. In consideration of the ups and downs I was navigating, I had to learn how to be more flexible than ever. Subsequently, I had to constantly better myself in all areas of my life. Even though I had a life, education, and employment experience prior coming to America, I had to start my life again, utterly from scratch.

As I was adjusting to my new environment and living with my host family, one morning as autumn leaves were falling in cascade onto the ground and the days were starting to get chilly, Kaleen and I went to the bank to open a student checking account for me. While we were at the bank, we overheard a tall gentleman with mysterious green eyes and dark hair talking to a cashier in French. Just as the gentleman was leaving the bank, Kayleen engaged in a conversation with him because he was a French speaker like me. He stated that his name was Seth. A few minutes into the conversation, he exchanged phone numbers with Kaleen. After some time, Kaleen and I were having a fun conversation, and when she asked me if Seth had called me at home, I said "no." At that time, Kaleen suggested that I call Seth. A few days later, I did. Eventually, Seth and I started going on dates. A couple of months later, Seth became my boyfriend. At the end of my English studies, I went back to Gabon for two months or so. Soon afterward and under another visa, I was back in the States to start business school for my executive assistant degree. This time, Seth and I were now living in the same home.

As a fervent believer in God, I believed that Seth was the man God had in mind for me. Seth was born in America in the state of Indiana when his parents lived and worked there for a short period. At one point, his parents returned to their native city of Montreal, Canada, when Seth was still an infant. Subsequently, Seth grew up in Montreal and was therefore fluent in both French and English. At the time of our meeting, Seth, who was seventeen years older than I, was working for the city of Rivere in Massachusetts and was responsible for the Management Information System Department. As our friendship and relationship developed, he became an essential person in my life. He was the one who translated my conversations to others when we went to stores and other public places. During the course of our relationship, he was always attentive to my emotional needs, and he invested time in me. He drove me places, we did many things together, traveling often, and we had fun being together. However, with Seth, I did not have the same type of financial freedom and security as I had with Alain. At the beginning of our relationship, there were a few times Seth had financial difficulties, and I had to help him pay a few bills; however, when he switched employment for higher pay this issue was resolved.

I had a deep affection for Seth. I wanted us to get married, but he was not interested in marriage with me and perhaps with no one else as he has remained single up to today. After five years of cohabiting with Seth and considering his reservations about commitment, I made the choice to leave him. My decision was also influenced in part by the fact that I was still under my student visa which was limiting my long-term stay in America. After considerable thought, I went back to Gabon as I did not really have anything tying me to the United States at that time. I remember how, on the day of my scheduled trip back to Gabon, Seth spent it crying inconsolably. No man has ever cried for me like that. It was a sad day for both of us. In fact, my separation from Seth was one of the hardest decisions I have ever had to make. The break-up affected me emotionally to the point that I remained single for quite a few years.

CHAPTER 8

ADVERSITIES AND MILESTONES

While back in Gabon, I worked for a couple of months or so for a renowned bank as an assistant to the Director of Human Resources. Following this, I started a position as a Secretary with the United Nations High Commissioner for Refugees (UNHCR), which I held for a few years. I enjoyed my work with UNHCR because I was directly involved in assisting refugees coming from war zones in Africa: from countries such as the Republic of Congo as well as others who were seeking asylum in Gabon and western countries. When I was a teenager, one of my dreams was to work for an international organization with a worldwide reputation such as the UNHCR, and now that dream was fulfilled.

Even though I enjoyed working with people and doing gratifying work, I also had the desire to further my education—specifically a bachelor's degree in social services as I wanted to work in a field that would help people in some way.

After a few years of working for the UNHCR and knowing that I was ready to go back to the US, I requested that my contract not be renewed for another year. So, at the end of my contract, I flew to the United States. Since Seth and I were still communicating, I went back to live with him for a second time, but this time only as a roommate.

I had an active savings account with an American bank, and I also was returning to the same business school where I had previously received my executive assistant certificate. This time it was to complete an associate degree. I believe that all these elements coupled with the fact of having a record of supporting myself in the United States in previous years helped me to re-enter the country without any difficulties. In fact, this was my third time to be granted a student visa to study in the United States.

During our relationship, Seth always had encouraged me to pursue higher education: he stated, "I would not be surprised to see you graduate with a college degree from one of the American universities." I believe that Seth's words of encouragement motivated me and built a confidence that I lacked with my limited English to pursue higher education and to earn multiple degrees after completion of my English language training.

After completion of my associate degree and having left Seth's home for the second time, I moved to the state of Indiana. One day, while riding on the bus, I met a middle-aged, well-educated Caucasian woman who started a conversation with me. Later on, down the road, we became friends. On one occasion, during our conversations, I expressed my desire to her to pursue my full college education. Soon after, she invited me to attend the Mennonite church where she was a member. During my visit to the church, she introduced me to the church's pastor. After that, I would sometimes attend church there, and on one Sunday, I came across a brochure with information about Goshen college. With the encouragement of my friend, I sought to learn more about Goshen college.

At age 38, while in Indianapolis, I enrolled in Goshen College, a private Mennonite college, to complete my bachelor's degree. Since I was returning to school, I went back to Gabon for a short period of time to get my school papers ready and to visit with my family—it was the fourth time I was attending an American school to study again.

Prior to attending college, I was confronted by friends who attended the same church. I was told by them that going away to college would have a negative impact on my Christian beliefs as I was cutting ties with the church of which I had been a member for quite a few years. At times, I felt that I was being lectured simply because I was determined to pursue my life's goals and objectives regardless of the obstacles.

In America, as a foreign-born, I have encountered some people who have mocked me because of my accent and others who have commented on it either in a positive or negative way. During my last year of college, as a part of the curriculum and required internship, I went to work for a nonprofit called Interfaith Hospitality that cared for the homeless in the town of Goshen. My tasks at the nonprofit consisted of assessing clients' problems and finding solutions to empower their lives. During those assessments, I was struggling with some of the stories I was hearing from these people who were desperate and hopeless. At times, it was emotionally draining but I also felt comfort in knowing that I was doing an assignment to help find solutions to their problems.

The director of that nonprofit organization was a male Caucasian. Throughout the internship, I never received feedback from him. Yet, upon reaching the end of my internship, I was told that my internship had not gone in a satisfactory way. My school counselor advised me to make last-minute changes to my degree to graduate from college. The whole situation made me feel baseless and inadequate. I remember how upset I was with the director: I felt humiliated and believed I had wasted my time. I could not fathom the whole situation. In the end, the school found an alternative organization for me to complete my internship.

When I shared my experience with my inner circle about the nonprofit organization and what had happened to me, many believed that the director of that organization was biased and treated me unfairly because of my race and place of origin. After that incident, the school reported to me that they were not going to place future students with that organization—especially students coming from foreign countries. This is the one situation in my life that made me really think hard about racism and discrimination in the United States. When I was growing up in Gabon, I had never experienced unfair treatment because my family's roots and ancestors come from royalty back in the colonial times. And, while I was in college, I have also experienced the generosity of many people who supported me through my journey as a college student from another country. I will forever be grateful for all the blessings.

Since I have been in this country, I have had my share of challenges because I have at times been evaluated and judged by the way I speak, especially in the workforce. I have always felt that some people have preconceived beliefs about foreigners: specifically, that they may not have the ability to adequately perform certain tasks. Once I was working for a tiny financial investment company where the owner was also interested in me in a romantic way. In fact, before we started working together, we were friends for a few years. Since the beginning of my employment with the company, I was always asked to do the tasks that no one else wanted to do. At times when I was talking to my boss, who also was a friend, he used derogatory words against me if we did not agree on certain issues. At that employment, I experienced moments where my opinions were not taken into consideration when I voiced them, and I was not trusted with information I was supposed to have to adequately perform my daily tasks. When I left the job, my employer refused to pay my retirement contribution which I was entitled to receive. In the end, I had to take legal action against him. I have confidence that this sort of mistreatment was exhibited toward me because of my origin.

At other times, I have had acquaintances and men interested by me in a romantic way who have asked me if I was "legal" in the United States as well as co-workers asking me if I were paying taxes. When you have people asking these types of questions, it just reinforces the beliefs and bias some people have about foreigners and their lack of knowledge about the immigration laws in this country.

After having experienced what I have had with my immigration status in this country, it is a situation that is very delicate and intricate to go through—I would say that each case is unique and that there is no fit-all solution. As we always hear, to comprehend one life's problems one has to go through them oneself: until it happens one would not be able to have compassion.

While I was in Goshen, I had student friends that were less than half my age, closer to the ages of my nieces and nephews. Nevertheless, I spent time interacting with these students; we had fun together through parties and get-togethers. It was always interesting to be around students from all walks of life and different cultures. Although I was a little more mature in age and wisdom, I also fit into their environment because of my youthful look, outgoing ways, and friendly personality.

Throughout the course of my studies, I eventually faced financial hardship as I was paying tuition from the personal savings I had accumulated from past employment when I was allowed to have a job with work visas. As a student from a foreign country, I was not eligible for government loans, but I was able to benefit from a little grant money from Goshen.

Halfway through the course of my studies, there was a time when I could not come up with the money for the tuition, and I was told by the school that I was going to be sent back to my country of origin if I was not able to continue paying the tuition. On that particular day, I was hopeless. After school, when I was in my tiny apartment, I cried out to God to come to my rescue as I did not know what my future would hold if I had to drop out of college. Although I was studying full-time with a heavy load of daily homework and was also working two part-time student jobs at the college to supplement my income, it was still not enough to pay all my expenses. Due to this, I was seeking monetary assistance from friends, my sister, nonprofit organizations, and anybody I knew who was willing to help.

While I was navigating these struggles and uncertainties with my schooling, I also experienced the hand of God working miracles through the few people and entities I mentioned above who helped me a little bit at times to make my dream of attaining a college degree come to pass. I still remember the day of my graduation: how surreal my accomplishments seemed! Even the college staff were amazed as they saw how challenging it had been for me to study in a language that was not native to me and to come up with the money for each semester.

Although it had taken me many years, a lot of money, effort, and determination, I achieved more than I could have imagined or thought possible for me to do. Perhaps one day by God's grace, I will complete a master's degree program.

CHAPTER 9

ANOTHER TRY AT LOVE

From an early age, my hope and dream has always been to be with a man I find enticing, to get married, and to stay committed to my marriage for the rest of my life.

At age 42, I was in my senior year in Goshen college when Gee found me on a Christian dating website and reached out to me. Gee was born and raised in Indiana and worked as a microbiologist for a renowned pharmaceutical company in Michigan. Since I have strong spiritual beliefs, one of the desires of my heart was to be with someone who shared my Christian faith. Albeit the fact that it took me several years searching for Mr.

Right, I praised God for having answered my prayers for Gee as he physically resembled the man I had always wanted to have in my life. Gee was tremendously good-looking with forget-me-not blue eyes, but, sad to say, his soul was big-time troubled.

At the beginning of our relationship, I was living in Goshen, and he was living in Kalamazoo, Michigan. Therefore, we would visit each other on weekends. At times, he would also visit me on weekdays as we were only living an hour away from each other. Little by little, I started to notice that if he saw me talking to any other male, even a classmate, he would get jealous. Once when I was visiting him in his state, we went shopping at the mall. When two men that I did not even know said "Hi" to me, he became bothered. He immediately told me that since I was not familiar with the place in which he lived, I should refrain from talking to the people there. He went on to say, "I know that you are a nice person, but I don't want you to be nice to people because I don't like it when people talk to you." Naively, I took his behavior for the expression of his love and care for me.

After I was graduated from college, I moved to Michigan to be with Gee. As we both were young and physically nice-looking, we were passionately attracted to each other. I remember how we always said that we would be together for the rest of our lives. Yet, during that period, I noticed that Gee was ambivalent whenever he had to make a decision. He also had frequent mood swings. Back then, I did not make much of it as

I attributed these things to insecurities that he was still battling as a result of the failure of his first marriage. I also secretly hoped that with time, as he conquered his uncertainties, his behavior would change for the better.

Within a few months, one morning he asked me to marry him. I said yes. Therefore, we went to Indiana, got married, and came back to Michigan late in the same day. Unfortunately, it did not take long for my marital life with Gee to turn into a real emotional roller-coaster.

Gee and I did not have a social life because he demanded that I no longer communicate or stay in touch with friends that I had known for several years before him; as he put it, he did not know them and did not want me to have my own friends. Besides, he did not introduce me to his friends simply because he did not have any. Therefore, we always spent our free time together.

At some point, he installed a key logger into my laptop unbeknownst to me, hacked into my email accounts, and deleted all male names on my contact list. When I discovered what he had done, I asked him to remove the electronic device from my computer, and he did. He explained to me that he was checking to see if I was pursuing a relationship with other men on the internet. After that incident, my computer never worked properly again. Consequently, I had to take it to several specialists and pay a significant amount of money to have it repaired.

In another instance, Gee allowed his parents to interfere in our relationship: they told him that since I was from Africa, I should get tested for HIV/AIDS because they did not trust people from Africa. I was in great shock to realize that Gee was so disingenuous that he would not tell his parents the truth. The truth was, and he knew it, that it was my habit to get tested for sexually transmitted diseases regularly, when I went through my physical exam every year or when I entered into a new relationship with a man. Also, I could not understand his reasons for not telling his parents that I had demanded he take the same medical tests for sexually transmitted diseases at the very beginning of our relationship and that, ironically, he had rejected my plea. What is more, his parents threatened to report me to the immigration services because their son had married me outside of their presence.

To make matters worse, Gee proved himself to be a sex addict. He demanded to have sex with me every single day at various times and in different ways, some of which I did not enjoy at all. Whenever I expressed some reservations to engage in certain kinds of sex, he would become very insensitive. Then, he would compare me to his ex-wife, who in his words, did not have any problems with such kinds of sex and used to give him full satisfaction by doing it wholeheartedly. One day he told me that if we were to have a child, that it would take away my constant availability for him to enjoy sexual pleasures with me. I was shocked by such a selfish statement. These were just a few of the erratic behaviors Gee exhibited. As days passed, it became obvious to me that the whole relationship was all about him, his personal needs, and that he was mentally instable coupled with compulsive control issues.

Another horror was that Gee's former wife, resentful of our relationship, attempted to poison us with cleaning chemicals by pouring them inside of our coffee machine. Per Gee's accounts, she also was suffering from mental illness.

On several occasions, I opened up to Gee about my feelings and asked him to change his controlling behavior as I expected better treatment from him. This whole ordeal was causing me a great deal of psychological distress as I was feeling powerless, betrayed, trapped, hurt, and had lost trust in Gee. In spite of all, I remembered my marriage and the vows I had uttered to my husband.

The last blow came about when, only a few months after we were married, Gee made the unilateral decision to have a vasectomy without talking to me about his intentions. After the operation, I was so devastated that I refused to be sexually intimate with him. A few days later he said to me that he had talked to his lawyer and had filed for divorce. Since I was already aching and mentally fatigued by his comportment, I did not have the desire to further discuss anything about the decisions he was making. Even though I had always believed that I was going to be happily married for only one time in my lifetime, at that moment, I just thanked God that my husband had filed for divorce.

I was in disbelief when, during the period that our divorce was in process, he would call me to ask for sex. One day he said to me, "you are still my wife, and I can have sex with you whenever I want." In the end, he wanted us to reconcile and work on our marriage, but

I forthrightly refused. Since Michigan is a "no fault" state, I felt liberated and serene after the divorce was final, and I was ready to move forward with my life.

In hindsight, after all the dramatic set of trials I endured with Gee were over, I realized that I was not well prepared or educated on the difficulties of mental illness in a romantic relationship and how to deal with it. Therefore, I sought psychological and spiritual assistance, for I was very weary, emotionally and physically. Even though the abuse was mainly emotional, it reminded me of the harm I had experienced from men in Gabon. However, this was the only relationship I had where the man I lived with totally invaded my privacy.

A friend of mine who was my confident prayed for me and Gee and for our relationship. My prayers were answered through divorce.

CHAPTER 10

NEW LOSSES AND PAINS

Over the last few years, life has brought more family tragedies.

In December 2012, I lost my beloved older sister, Britt, from cancer. My sister's death was devastating because we always had a very close relationship. The day I was informed of my sister's death, I felt like I had been stabbed in my chest, and I could not sleep for two days. The first night of her passing, a sister from a church I was attending at the time stayed on the phone with me during the entire night. My heart was in such pain and was suffering palpitations. At some point, I thought I was going to die too. The pain I felt was unbearable and excruciating. As I was also in the process of the divorce from Gee, it was just a lot to endure alone.

After her passing, my family and I had to step in to take care of the five children she left behind. This unexpected situation has been overwhelming as I have become a mother to my nieces and nephews by guiding and helping them daily with all their needs. My sister was married for almost twenty years, but all through the last years of her life, she was separated from her husband because of physical and verbal abuse. I still remember the conversations I had with my sister about domestic violence in a relationship and how I had influenced her decision to leave her abusive husband. In the end, I was relieved to see my sister moving forward with her life as a single mother, exceling in her career, and pursuing her life's goals.

As she was living her new life, she was also battling cancer and fighting her ex-husband in court for child support. Up to the time of her passing, she was never granted child support even though four of her children were living with her in her new home. In addition, my sister's divorce was never finalized as she encountered some obstacles from the judicial system, which is not always in favor of women. In fact, she was asked to find ways to resolve the marital issues with her estranged husband on her own. She never received a dime from her husband to help support her children, and in the end, she died from the disease that was destroying her body.

At times, when I think of my sister, I am overwhelmingly saddened and angered at all she had to go through

THE COURAGE TO LEAVE

during the last years of her time on earth. As of today, my sister's children are now young adults and all are thriving on their owns ways, with the exception of the youngest who still is a minor and needs family assistance.

In December 2016, in parallel manner to her deceased mother, my niece Joanna was involved in a domestic violence dispute with her former boyfriend. As the result of this dispute, Joanna was hospitalized and in a coma on an intensive care unit for two months; the confrontation with her former boyfriend left her paralyzed for two years. This incident was distressing for the entire family and got me even closer to God as I was praying at all times, every single day, for my niece. Up to today, Joanna is still suffering emotional, physical, and health problems due to that incident. Since innovation in medicine in certain fields is still lacking in Gabon, no one has been able to pinpoint the real cause of Joanna's ailments. In addition, the former boyfriend was never prosecuted for his vicious behavior toward Joanna as she did not report the case to law enforcement. On top of that, the former boyfriend is a member of the judicial system in Gabon. Given his social position, I believe Joanna would have faced enormous barriers or hostility for her to get justice.

In November 2018, my father left this world due to complications related to his diabetes. Before he died, my father asked for forgiveness for not having been the father who cared for and financially supported his children. He acknowledged having missed out on many opportunities for having a loving and solid relationship with his children. On one hand, I was saddened by his passing; on the other hand, I was never emotionally connected to him as I have never felt like he was my father. In my head, I always know I have his last name on my birth certificate and other identification cards, but my real parents always were my maternal grandparents who raised me because I loved them deeply.

In May 2021, again my family was devasted by the death of my little sister, Ina. Although for some years now Ina had been dealing with some health issues that were caused by her husband's infidelities, it did not appear to us that her health was deteriorating. During my routine conversations with Ina, I always asked if she was following her daily medication treatments, and she always said, "sure I am." I trusted her.

In the last four months of her life, she changed and did not want to communicate with me and the family. She was always finding an excuse to avoid talking with the family in her last days. As a family, we did not understand. Now that she is gone, we suspect that Ina was suffering in silence and was trapped in a controlling marriage. As the family is grappling with the reality of her passing, we believe that she was emotionally manipulated by her husband to the point that she must have been giving up her daily medications. The problem is that she never talked about her marital troubles to the family. My family and I have been puzzled by her unexpected death and do not have answers. My family does not wish to prosecute the husband, as it would be difficult to prove allegations of abuse as we have no concrete proof. In addition, Ina is the mother of eight

THE COURAGE TO LEAVE

children, and her husband has always been the sole financial provider of the family. Prosecuting him would complicate the lives of the children.

When losses and unforeseen life events happen, it is burdensome to deal with them as it causes discomfort and all kinds of feelings; but over time, we are usually able to find comfort and peace although the situation may still be painful at times. Sometimes, I want things to be like when I was a child without complications and obstructions; nevertheless, as we age, most things in life do become harder.

After Ina's death, I once again felt powerless because I did not help my sister as I had wished to do, being physically far away from my family. I am in pain for my sisters' deaths, which have made me ponder life and its significance. Simultaneously, a deep desire to create an education program that would empower women to take control of their own lives and contribute to Gabon society in all forms has been growing in my mind.

From time to time, I have conversations with acquaintances living in Gabon and have learned that society has normalized and institutionalized abusive behavior toward women. Now, more than ever, women believe "abuse" to be not only acceptable but an affirmation of "being loved" by men. I worry about the way women are being brainwashed daily and are not educated on the issues of "abuse" and "male domination."

CHAPTER 11

NEW ASPIRATIONS

As time has passed bringing more experience, I have evolved in so many ways even though I am still going through personal challenges.

In terms of my love life, the desire of my heart is still to be in a faithful, loving, and healthy relationship with a gentleman who will value our relationship, enjoy our company, and grow old with me. I have been diligently praying and on the lookout for my life' partner for some time now.

So far, the men who are attracted to me often, though they may say otherwise, have no genuine desire to commit to a long-term relationship. As a consequence, whenever I meet a man and I see that the relationship is not going in that direction, I always have to say goodbye in order to protect my own mental and physical health. Dealing with men who are wishy-washy can be time consuming and emotionally stressful. For that reason and on occasion, I no longer have the same longing for a relationship with a man because I have become increasingly annoyed and disappointed with the many issues involved with dating around here.

It has been a struggle to find a gentleman whose life's desires, goals, and values are aligned with mine and who is not ambivalent about his love for me. Believe or not, a few years ago, I crossed the path of a man who was interested by me romantically but struggled to be with me because I was Black.

He was so concerned about the opinions of people. It was a weird statement for me to hear in the 21st century in America.

My desire for a child has been a continuing dilemma as the men I have been in an intimate relationship with either cannot have children because they have had a vasectomy or do not wish to have more children. Yet I do not want to give up on my dream of being a mother as it is so deeply ingrained in me. At present, I have been exploring diverse paths to becoming a mother. During my entire adult life, I have dealt with some health issues in my reproductive system because of dysmenorrhea. Simultaneously, I am also battling fears of my own in becoming a single mother. I always have hoped to be in a steadfast and loving relationship by now and have a family with my special gentleman. Still, I am not going to give up on the desires of my heart. In some ways I have "mothered" others, but I am still not the mother I always have wanted to be. My experiences in Gabon taught me the importance of having children and of taking good care of them. I do not want to be with a gentleman who would not consider having a child in his life.

Nowadays, I am living a little bit more spontaneously which pleases me. For so many years, I have been making life choices according to the circumstances I have been facing on a day-to-day basis. Thus far, I do not regret the decisions I have made because they were necessary and worthwhile although some others have also negatively impacted my life's aspirations.

As I am now in the full bloom of age (50), I have become more health conscious: I pay attention to the food I eat and any products I use on my body. I am not a *cordon bleu* as my grandmother was, but I do cook from scratch and my food tastes delicious most times. I am very creative with my cooking and use a variety of strategies when I cook. I usually don't totally follow a recipe as I like to add my own touch to things. My grandmother used to cook with her "eyes" since she never owned or bought cooking books, and I use the same technique when I cook.

I also am a naturalist and I like to be out to smell the fresh air and explore nature. I like the serenity that emanates from the trees and vegetation when I am in the open air.

In term of my professional ambitions, I always have had an idea on the type of work that interests me and would provide me with emotional gratification. Unfortunately for years and up to this point, I mostly have worked jobs that I haven't enjoyed much but I had to do them in order to pay my bills. At the same time, some of those jobs did not pay a livable salary, and I have often struggled to make ends meets.

This reinforces the reality that, for an immigrant, life is not always easy as some people may think it is. Sometimes, one has to work harder at almost everything and do some of the jobs that some people born in this country don't want to do in order to survive. This can be especially challenging for an immigrant who has no family ties in this country.

As I have earned substantial work experience and higher education, I now am seeking jobs that are more pleasing to perform and emotionally fulfilling to me. The jobs I have most enjoyed are those where I closely worked with needy people. I would like to utilize the skills I have acquired to create my own employment.

I believe that I was born with a caring heart as I am good at listening to people's problems, and I have special abilities when it comes to giving advice. For many years now, when I interact and communicate with strangers, acquaintances, and family, I find that I connect with them on a deep level to the point that I can sense certain situations that are going on with them. Oftentimes, I am able to guide them to find solutions.

While living in the United States, I have experienced both the goodwill and the malice of people. I grew up in a household where violence was not in my family's values and upbringing, and yet I was assaulted by wicked human beings. Since I have been living in the United States, I have learned more about certain issues impacting humanity. I have learned how to put myself in another person's shoes and have more empathy. I value people and life because God created each person for a specific purpose and reason.

Taking all this into consideration, I would like to become a women's "keeper": to help the ones who have been suffering for generation after generation from all sorts of abuse from men, especially in Gabon. I am also interested in having an impact on the legal system that continues to impede women's rights. I am not certain what my future holds, but I trust God with decisions I make and things I do.

I have always believed that it is the blessing of God who touched the heart of Alain to help me come to the United States of America to learn a new language, to be empowered with valuable education and work experience, and live differently. Being an immigrant and a citizen of this country, I now have experienced two different ways of life, which is an asset that would benefit women in Gabon whom I would like to help educate on the issue of domestic violence in relationship with men.

EPILOGUE

These days I have the desire to visit my family. My mother is retired and is getting older, and it would be nice for me to see her and the rest of my extended family. As I am getting mature in age, I am thinking more about my roots and family. The course of my life did not go as I thought it would have gone. Each day of my life, I am learning to live with circumstances that cross my path and which are beyond my control. We live in a world where multiple forces can act in a bad or good way in one's life.

There were times when I was discouraged and ready to give up. At the same time, I have lived the last twenty years of my life trusting that God has something for me here which I will continue to pursue, no matter the impediments.

Throughout the years, I have learned to be patient, vulnerable, humble, more compassionate, more understanding, and more accepting of life's setbacks while being grateful for the successes I have achieved as well as the life I have lived although not picture-perfect.

ACKNOWLEDGMENTS

B ritt and Ina, you have given me more motivation to write this segment of my life's story and share it with the world. You are always loved and forever engraved in my memory. I miss you both a lot, and I am in pain.

I would like to thank all the people that God has put in my path since I have been in this country and who have helped me in any way through difficult situations. For each situation I have traversed, God always has sent somebody to give me a hand even when I did not know where the help would come from.

Although I don't have family in this country, I have friends that always have been a support to me. I am grateful to all people who have contributed to my life and continue to do so in any ways.

To all the people who are going through difficult times, there is always a way at the end of the tunnel: have faith.

Life teaches us everything; whether good or bad, what we learn is unpredictable. I have been a never-ending student of life.

Special thanks to the man who allowed me to first come in the United States; without your opening this opportunity to me, I would not have been able to write this book and make it known to the public.

My family love to you all!

Made in the USA
Monee, IL
08 March 2024